The Winning Welcome

The Winning Welcome

*Helping Church Newcomers
Feel at Home*

by
Sharon Bushey

Beacon Hill Press of Kansas City
Kansas City, Missouri

ISBN: 083-411-3252

Printed in the
United States of America

Cover Design: Paul Franitza

10   9   8   7   6   5   4   3   2

I lovingly dedicate this book
to my parents,
Udell and Doris Moss,
whose love and enthusiasm for sharing Christ
continue to impact my life.

November 1950. Rev. Udell Moss welcomes his
daughter, Sharon (the author), to the first service of
the newly organized Church of the Nazarene in Ferguson, Mo.

Foreword

After my recent travels to Korea, I returned to America feeling that we knew very little about making people feel welcomed, wanted, and comfortable in our churches. We were saying, "Help yourself," instead of "Here, let me help you."

I was encouraged to discover, however, that someone else had sensed the frustrations I felt and has written a resourceful, delightful book to help churches remedy the problem. In *The Winning Welcome,* Sharon Bushey describes my frustration with literature tables, programs, and other items void of personal assistance. Then she gives tried solutions to end these frustrations. Making our visitors feel welcome does not happen automatically. We must plan for the arrival of the newcomer and, as Mrs. Bushey and her family did, put ourselves into the shoes of the newcomer and remember how it feels to be new.

This book is an organized plan for making your welcome one that wins the newcomer to yourselves, your church, and your Christ. The methods are vividly reinforced by personal anecdotes from the author's storehouse of parsonage memories.

I recommend this book not only for greeters and ushers but for any pastor or layman who wants to reach out to the newcomer in a more effective way, thereby following Christ's admonition to "produce fruit that will last." Your church needs *The Winning Welcome* and it can begin with you.

—BILL M. SULLIVAN, *Director*
Church Growth Division
Church of the Nazarene

Preface

Although family vacations are a time to explore new scenery, new restaurants, and new attractions, the adventuresome spirit quickly dwindles, however, as we approach the inevitable Sunday excursions. Our three adolescents, ages 17, 14, and 12, have attended Sunday School and church since the week following their births. They know their Bible stories and are adept on theological questions. Why then all the hassle over attending church during vacation?

When I asked the family during a recent vacation about their fears, they were quick with these responses. "We don't like being the new person." (Fear of feeling ignored or alone.) "We don't know where to find our class or find you when it's over." (Fear of being lost or looking dumb.) "They might ask me a question that I don't know how to answer." (Fear of embarrassment.)

Our offspring were easily convinced that their complaining was futile. We would go to Sunday School and church, even on vacation. Their expressed fears, however, heightened my awareness of what visitors face when coming to our church. So we approached vacation Sundays with pen in hand, determined to learn how to ease the pain of being a visitor. Thus the desire to write this book was born.

Part 1, The Royal Welcome, will challenge you to make your church a place where visitors are comfortable. These chapters will help you analyze your present greeting ministry, will give you possibilities for expansion and improvement, and will also give some simple guidelines for favorably impressing the newcomer with yourself and your church.

Part 2, Feeling at Home, will challenge you to go beyond The Royal Welcome. Although newcomers may decide to attend your church regularly because of the royal welcome, they will soon feel unwelcome and will cease attending if they are not adequately integrated into the life of your church.

Although all greeters and ushers will not be involved in the organization and implementation of all of the suggested ministries listed in these chapters, hopefully you will support them with your prayers.

In these pages I hope that you will find simple guidelines and instruction and will also be challenged to make your church not only a place where visitors are comfortable and desire to return but also a place where they can feel at home.

1

Within the Comfort Zone

In everything, do to others what you would have them do to you (Matt. 7:12).

* * * * *

And if you greet only your brothers, what are you doing more than others? Do not even pagans do that? (Matt. 5:47).

* * * * *

Then he said to his disciples, "The harvest is plentiful but the workers are few. Ask the Lord of the harvest, therefore, to send out workers into his harvest field" (Matt. 9:37-38).

* * * * *

A new command I give you: Love one another. As I have loved you, so you must love one another. . . . all men will know that you are my disciples, if you love one another (John 13:34-35).

* * * * *

My purpose is that they may be encouraged in heart and united in love, so that they may have the full riches of complete understanding, in order that they may know the mystery of God, namely, Christ, in whom are hidden all the treasures of wisdom and knowledge (Col. 2:2-3).

11

By the time I was two years old, my father had completed a term in evangelism and had been convinced by a layman and the Lord to begin a church in Ferguson, Mo. My earliest recollections of that ministry are of riding a Cushman motor scooter with my father, inviting people to church.

The church was literally our home since it had been constructed to accommodate the parsonage family in an upper room apartment. It was common for my brother and me to play church and talk church wherever we were. As a child I was always comfortable at church.

Most parsonage families move several times during the growing years of the children, but my father was one of those unusual men who pastored his first and only church for 31 years. Therefore I remained comfortable: I never changed churches, never changed school districts, and never was forced to be the newcomer.

Perhaps in search of the unfamiliar, I was ready to forsake comfort when it was time to choose a college. My choice led me 500 miles from home to a college off of our church's educational zone where I knew almost no one.

I remember deciding to try several of the local churches. I was especially intrigued by the one that had a bus to transport college students to each of the services several miles across town. I decided to try it first, reasoning that it must offer something that made it worth the ride.

Although this was the first time in my life to be the newcomer, I was prepared to search for acceptance and to initiate friendliness. Every Sunday, though, only heightened my awareness that I was struggling unsuccessfully for a place in an already established group. My smiles were not returned, and my offers to help were not accepted. I soon came to the conclusion that you had to have already known someone before coming to this church in order to be accepted.

Deciding that being the newcomer was too painful, I forsook my church search and attended a large church within walking distance of the college. There I slipped into a worship habit completely void of fellowship. Apparently no one seemed to know when I was there, nor miss me when I was sick.

After marriage and college days, my husband was asked to be the youth minister at my home church in Ferguson. Back to the comfort of home. I was glad not to have to experience the pain of being a newcomer.

After six years in comfort, my husband was asked to begin a new church in Waynesville, Mo., only three hours from our home. Technically I was a newcomer, but since the church was small, and everyone was new, I easily found a place of comfort, a place of acceptance, and a place of automatic ministry.

God must have seen what was becoming of me after the extended years of comfort, for after five years in that comfortable home mission situation, He abruptly shook me from the nest. We moved 700 miles away from family and friends to a large, 52-year-old church that still had charter members attending. I was definitely the newcomer.

How well I remember the months of inner struggle as I searched for smiles and friendship and acceptance. All the positions in the church were adequately filled without my expertise. It took almost a year to find my place of ministry and to feel at home in this congregation, but at last I became comfortable again.

And so it was that our recent vacations were a reminder that I had found a place of ministry, had found friends, and had settled once again into comfort within our church. Our vacation Sunday excursions also reminded me that after having gained comfort, I had seemingly lost empathy with the fears of the newcomer. Our family's resistance to attending church on vacation was the catalyst to reawaken my awareness of the newcomer's fears and needs.

We approached the inevitable vacation Sunday excursions with pen in hand, determined to learn firsthand about being a fearful visitor. For our benefit we would also pretend that we were in search of a new church home. Those Sunday excursions led us to four churches of varied sizes and of three different denominations. At the end of the vacation Sundays, we theoretically chose which church we would like to attend.

As you read our observations, ask yourself, What is important to newcomers? What determines whether or not they will return to my church a second Sunday? And, if you were the newcomer in search of a church, which of these churches would you choose to attend?

Church A

We chose not to attend Sunday School but only to attend worship service on the first Sunday of vacation. The young members of the family were delighted that we would enter our adventures gradually due to the injured foot of our daughter, Karen, that needed to be elevated as much as possible.

This particular morning we decided not to choose a church because of its name or reputation; rather we would choose one that "looked inviting." After driving for several miles through an affluent residential area, we visually inspected a lovely, new brick church. The landscaping, the building, and the lighted glass sign all said, "Welcome." The spacious parking lot made it convenient to unload crutches and kids. We would worship here.

Several other families arrived as we did. "They must be visitors, too," our crew remarked, for they stared straight ahead and never gave us a glance.

We entered the crowded foyer, trying desperately to protect Karen's foot as we were bumped and jostled by a noisy mob. They were obviously enjoying one another but didn't seem to notice us. We felt alone even though we were surrounded by people.

By trial and error we discovered the coatracks and assumed that the sanctuary must be in the direction of the pushing crowd. An usher met us at the sanctuary door and escorted us to a seat with no verbal exchange. I guess he assumed that he knew where we wanted to sit and that the bulletin he had given us contained sufficient information for the service.

We followed the program, enjoyed the minister's sermon, and were assured by the bulletin inserts that this was a fairly small but active church with much to offer our family. We asked ourselves, "If we lived in this community, would we want to come again to take advantage of these ministries?" Not likely. No one spoke to us or even sent a smile in our direction. We felt like intruders, and that's not a pleasant experience that anyone wants to repeat.

Church B

For our second adventure we chose a church because of reputation. We had heard that 2,500 people worshiped here weekly in three Sunday morning services. As far as we were concerned, they had two strikes against them before we arrived: (1) They were too large to be personable. (2) They had multiple services, a modern excuse for being aloof.

Upon arriving, we waited in line for at least 10 minutes for a parking space. Since others were waiting with us, we reasoned that this must be part of the weekly ritual. The early worshipers soon departed, and we took their place. Fearful that we'd never find the main entrance in the maze of buildings, we approached the nearest door. To our relief and amazement, even that door was staffed with greeters. We immediately sensed that they were expecting us and were prepared to eliminate our fears.

We were shown on a map where the young people's

classes were located. We were given a brief summary of the adult classes available and were offered assistance in choosing one. They even suggested that our oldest son might prefer to attend with us. How perceptive they were of a senior higher's apprehensions.

Our younger adolescents were welcomed by a greeter at their department. The time and place were set where we would be rejoined for worship. We all felt at ease.

Amazingly, we felt comfortable in our class of over 600. Their announcements, the coffee cup in most everyone's hand, the class discussion, and the openness of the teacher helped us to relax and caused us to want to return. I considered asking my husband for a sabbatical so that I could attend this class. It was large but definitely not impersonal.

Someone out of this huge class had the courage to ask if we were new, if we were staying for worship, and if we would like an escort through the maze of hallways to the sanctuary. With gratitude we said, "Most certainly." Before parting, she introduced us to an usher who escorted us to the seat of our choice.

The message was good, and their program proved that this was an active church with much to offer our family. Would waiting for a parking space and the awesomeness of this church's size keep us from returning a second Sunday? Not likely. We wanted to return because we had been positively affected by the friendliness of the people and the expertise of the greeters and ushers who relieved our fears by answering our questions before we asked.

Church C

Our vacation schedule brought us into the town of Church C on Saturday afternoon. We decided to use this extra time to peruse the facilities. We were awed by the beauty of Church C. As we gazed at this massive monument to God and architecture, we mentally were calculating the probable cost and man-hours involved. This large congregation had spent much to "make a statement" to their community. We were overwhelmed by their commitment.

The main entrance had an impressive Welcome Center stocked with informative brochures. Each auxiliary door had a small, attractively decorated welcome desk. Our camera clicked rapidly; we took notes and drew diagrams. We were impressed!

On Sunday morning we arrived just shortly before starting time. To expedite matters, since the parking lots were quite a distance away, my husband delivered the family to the side door where we hoped we would save time by getting information about the classes we would attend. We approached the beautifully decorated welcome desk, but no one was there. Several people passed during our wait, but no one spoke. Oh well, we knew our way around, so we decided to try the main entrance Welcome Center. We were sure that we'd find assistance there.

To our surprise only the words "Welcome" greeted us. The center was there, the brochures were there, but we needed a person to answer our questions. The Welcome Centers were definitely signs that a committee once upon a time had decided to prepare adequately for visitors. The absence of staff in these centers, however, spoke louder than their good intentions.

After scanning the foyer for a knowledgeable-looking face, we found an associate pastor seated at a desk. We asked for directions and were thereafter treated graciously. It seemed, however, that our arrival had surprised him.

In the Sunday School class, we were introduced along with other visitors, and we enjoyed the unique presentation of the lesson. Several lingered after class for fellowship, but we felt uncomfortable to stay, since we were not included in their conversations. We slipped out unnoticed, found the rest of our family, and made our way to the sanctuary.

The pastor gave a good message, and the bulletin undeniably described an active church with much to offer our family. We asked ourselves if we would want to return to this church if we lived in this community. Not likely. We were impressed by their beautiful structure and their adequate welcome facilities, but since absolutely no one spoke to us except the hired staff with whom we had initiated conversation, we did not feel welcome. We were glad that we didn't have to return to this church regularly.

Church D

Our final vacation adventure took us to another large church. Now, we're not prejudiced against small churches. We've grown up in some, been members of some, and even started one. We know that small churches can also choose to give their visitors a warm or cool reception, because the principles of friendliness apply to churches of all sizes. We believed, however, that it was even more probable that we would get lost in the shuffle and not be recognized in a larger church.

Bare lawns and construction equipment made it obvious that Church D was still in a building program. We parked and followed the families who were disappearing into the cluster of buildings.

In the central courtyard between the buildings, we spotted a Welcome Center. It was bustling with activity. We signed the register, received a visitor's identification flower, and were introduced to greeters who showed each of us to our classes. After class several couples seemed genuinely interested in knowing who we were. Their questions implied, "We'd really like to have the opportunity to know you better." Before and after the worship service, we had countless people notice our visitor I.D. and give us brief but warm greetings.

The pastor preached a good message, and the bulletin gave sufficient evidence that this was an active church that could meet the needs of our family; but it was the caring people who reached out to say, "Welcome," that caused us to wish that we could attend Church D regularly.

Which Church Does Your Visitor Find?

Could it be that the visitor who walks through your church doors is much like our family? Have they also come with fears and the need for friendliness? Are they fearing feeling alone or ignored? Are they fearing being lost in your facilities? Are they fearing embarrassment?

All the churches that we attended on our vacation Sunday excursions had an exceptionally good orator as their minister. They all advertised programs to meet the spiritual needs and social needs of our family. The summary of our visits, however, was that we would choose to attend a church where our fears were relieved and where we were welcomed warmly.

If we as a parsonage family felt the need to be loved, how much greater that need must be for a visitor who has no church background. His heart has drawn him to church and the things of God, but his head will convince him not to return unless he feels loved and welcomed.

Friendliness cannot be dictated, but it is a skill that a congregation can learn. By acknowledging your church's needs, by applying some tested guidelines of the "dos and don'ts," and by activating a simple organizational plan, your congregation can learn to welcome and care for your visitors effectively.

Action

Think About It

1. If you were choosing a church or were recommending a church to a friend, you would probably choose either Church B or Church D. What specific qualities determined your choice?

2. Churches, like people, have distinct personalities and make vivid first impressions. Reflect on the churches that you have attended. Specifically describe some of your first impressions, both favorable and unfavorable.

Do Something

1. Candidly interview a new person in your congregation. Ask them to express some honest first impressions of your church. Ask them for suggestions of how you could improve (or begin) your greeting program so that visiting your church would be a pleasant experience.

2. Ask an unchurched friend, "If you attended our church, what could we do that would help you to know that we cared for you and really wanted you to be a part of our fellowship?"

2

General Practitioner
or Specialist

I am sending you to them to open their eyes and turn them from darkness to light, and from the power of Satan to God, so that they may receive forgiveness of sins and a place among those who are sanctified by faith in me (Acts 26:17-18).

* * * * *

Serve wholeheartedly, as if you were serving the Lord, not men (Eph. 6:7).

* * * * *

I would rather be a doorkeeper in the house of my God than dwell in the tents of the wicked (Ps. 84:10).

* * * * *

You show that you are a letter from Christ, the result of our ministry, written not with ink but with the Spirit of the living God, not on tablets of stone but on tablets of human hearts (2 Cor. 3:3).

* * * * *

You are the salt of the earth. But if the salt loses its saltiness, how can it be made salty again? It is no longer good for anything, except to be thrown out and trampled by men. You are the light of the world. A city on a hill cannot be hidden. Neither do people light a lamp and put it under a bowl. Instead they put it on its stand, and it gives light to everyone in the house. In the same way, let your light shine before men, that they may see your good deeds and praise your Father in heaven (Matt. 5:13-16).

High school graduation was only a few weeks away, and I was feeling the need to meet the world. College and marriage both were in my plans, and both required money. It was obvious that a job was the first need. I submitted my résumé, small as it was, to almost every business in town.

To my delight the local bank hired me as a switchboard operator. The job would also require recounting tellers' money for bundling as well as opening safe-deposit boxes for customers during peak times. The description of the job sounded terrific when I was sitting across the desk from the man who did the hiring. I knew phone manners (although I'd never even seen a switchboard, let alone having operated one), knew how to count money (although allowances and baby-sitting money had never accumulated enough to open a bank account), and knew how to use a key to open locks (although I'd never used two keys at once or ever having seen inside a bank vault). Nevertheless, I was a confident senior.

Realizing that this would probably be my last vacation with the family, Father insisted that I go on vacation with them before starting the new job. While sitting on the shore of a beautiful lake in Minnesota, I thought about more than the clear, blue water. There were two weeks to evaluate this new career position and to reevaluate my adequacies. Two weeks were long enough to consider all the things that could possibly go wrong. Two weeks were long enough to reconsider my abilities as a senior. Perhaps I had oversold myself on that résumé.

Although a once-confident graduate, I approached the first day at work hoping frantically to survive at least one day in the work force. It was a relief to be offered assistance in every job upon arriving at the bank that hot, memorable summer morning. Lead questions were given to ask the callers; I was told the proper way to hold money in order to quickly sort, count, and bundle it; and someone promised to follow close behind until I became comfortable with the safe-deposit box procedures. The list of expectations for each job description and the available assistance were the crutches needed for my weak knees.

As you accept a position in the ministry of greeting within your church, you may also find your confidence dwindling. If so, encourage yourself to pursue this ministry. When my confidence and energy begin to wane, my commitment to involvement is renewed by remembering former President Reagan's famous words: "If not you, who? If not now, when?"

This chapter will offer answers to questions about the specific job descriptions of the greeters and ushers. Each position is described in detail. These descriptions can be used as your crutches for your weak knees.

The possible positions for greeters and ushers are many, and the list of their duties is lengthy. Just so you don't become overwhelmed before you finish this chapter, at the beginning determine whether your church is to be a specialist or a general practitioner. In the medical field small towns usually have a general practitioner. This one doctor delivers babies, removes tonsils and appendixes and whatever else ails you, and prescribes medications for everyone's aches and pains. This one man has to fulfill many responsibilities. The larger a city is, however, the more specialists it can boast of. One specialist treats only the heart, another only the feet, another only the skin, and another only the cornea of the eye. Each specialist serves many people but treats them only in the area of his expertise.

Larger churches, likewise, will probably use many people

to staff all of the following suggested greeter/usher positions. They will need to specialize just because of their size. The smaller church, on the other hand, may be able to begin their greeting ministry with only one or two greeters/ushers, who will be much like a general practitioner who covers the duties of several positions. Small church, don't become discouraged with the possibilities of specialization; rather, do your job well as a general practitioner while planning for growth and future specialization.

The Parking Lot and Portico Greeter

Visitors should feel welcome as soon as they enter your parking lot. Their first fear will be eliminated when you help them find a parking space. Your very presence will say, "We were expecting you to come today." As a parking lot greeter, you should give a friendly "hello" to everyone, members and visitors alike. You may be the first happy voice some people have heard yet that day. Your cheerfulness may create a foundational attitude for their worship.

It is not necessary for a parking lot greeter to introduce himself and ask the visitors to identify themselves. Situations may alter this, but it is usually best to keep your conversation to a minimum.

As a parking lot greeter, you should also assist the newcomers in finding the main entrance or the easiest entry to the church. You should prepare them for what they will find inside. Assure them that someone will be by the door to give them assistance.

Frequently a family member will transport the rest of the family to a service but will never come themselves. As a parking lot greeter, you can make the most of these opportunities by getting acquainted with these family members and, when appropriate, inviting them to join you in worship or fellowship. They may be curious to see inside your church but too fearful to make the first step into a new situation. If they feel that they already know you, they will have overcome the first barrier.

Always watch for those who need assistance. Take special care of the handicapped and the elderly, but don't neglect assisting young parents who are juggling kids, diaper bags, and Sunday School packets. Parking lot greeters may also assist with courtesy umbrellas on rainy days.

Some churches have a portico for the convenience of unloading passengers in inclement weather. Whether or not your church has a portico, if you have a place where attenders regularly unload before parking, a greeter should staff this position. This greeter would assume the same responsibilities as the parking lot greeters but would also assist by opening the vehicle and church doors when possible.

My uncle pastored a growing congregation in Ohio where the wife of a local, young business executive attended. His church had ministered effectively to this woman for over a year but had never convinced her husband to attend. Whenever my uncle made a pastoral call, the husband always responded with a belligerent "No, thank you!" He was too busy for God and the church. He'd let his wife come, but he didn't want to be bothered with religion.

The wife continued to come and be blessed by the fellowship of my uncle's church. A nearby church of a different denomination, however, had a special missionary speaker one evening whom the wife wanted to hear. She asked her husband to accompany her, and he gave his usual reply, "No, thank you! I'll take you, but I won't stay."

The young executive wasn't prepared, however, for the friendliness of the parking lot greeters at this church. He had dropped his wife off at my uncle's church for months and had never met anyone. This church was different.

Before he realized what was happening, someone was

opening the car door for his wife and showing him to a parking place. He tried to explain that he didn't plan to stay, but their friendly enthusiasm about what was going to take place inside enticed him. Since he was a salesman, he wanted to check out the product of their sales pitch.

To my uncle's dismay, the nearby church gained that young executive and his wife to their congregation because of some friendly parking lot greeters. My uncle often wondered if he could have had the pleasure of leading that man to the Lord if he had had a team of greeters in his parking lot.

You still may wonder if a parking lot and portico greeter position can be that important: just standing there directing traffic, smiling, opening doors, and assisting people with their belongings. Let me share this simple analogy.

We live in a small community with only three grocery stores. Each has a unique personality.

Store A is the closest, located right in the heart of the residential area. It is small, friendly, and family owned, but somewhat poorly stocked. I choose it when I am in a hurry.

Store B is only a few blocks further than Store A. It is known for its bargain prices and double-coupon redemption. However, the checkers are always disgruntled, and the baggers will begrudgingly assist you only if you insist. I go to that store when I'm pinching pennies, which is most of the time, but I dread every minute that I'm there.

Store C is several miles across town. It's not convenient, and it's not financially beneficial to go there. But if I need a bright spot in my week, I'll shop there just because of the atmosphere. The stock boys are courteous and helpful. The checkers are pleasant. The baggers insist on helping you with your bags. I feel special and feel that my business is appreciated when shopping in Store C.

It has been surprising lately to learn that many friends have also identified the unique personality of each store, and they shop in the three stores for the same reasons. Several have, however, made the permanent switch to Store C because they enjoy an atmosphere of friendliness, and they appreciate the help of the baggers.

If ladies feel that way about a grocery store, I just imagine that many of the people who are dropped off at the porticos of the churches in your community are evaluating the churches in much the same way. Many desire assistance, and some, because of circumstances, must have it. A greeter in your parking lot and at your portico can lend that helping hand.

Door and Foyer Greeters

Although most visitors will try to find the main entrance, or what appears to be the main entrance, they are known to enter the most unlikely doors of the church. Thus every entry should be staffed adequately with greeters. The auxiliary doors of your church should be staffed according to their normal amount of usage. If it is convenient, the visitors could be escorted from these doors to the main Welcome Center. The auxiliary greeter can then return to his post. A sufficient number of greeters is always needed at each door so that a door is never left unattended.

The main doors and foyer should be staffed with an adequate number of greeters to fill the following positions:
1. Door Greeter
2. Welcome Center Secretary
3. Welcome Center Host/Hostess
4. Escorts
5. Sanctuary Door Greeter

In a small church these could feasibly be handled by one person.

Door Greeter

A door greeter is a stationary greeter who welcomes everyone. The main responsibility of this greeter is to determine who are the visitors. (See chapter 3, Guideline 4.) After making brief introductions, the visitors should be directed to the Welcome Center host/hostess or to an auxiliary secretary desk for registration.

Welcome Center Secretary

The Welcome Center secretary should greet the visitors and ask them to sign the register. If you sense someone hesitating, perhaps that visitor is having flashbacks of previous churches and solicitors who have gotten his address and proceeded to hassle him for weeks and months with "junk mail" and pledge cards. If appropriate, relieve the visitors' fears by explaining your purpose for the register. Assure them that they will not be put on a mailing list, but that your pastor would just like to send a letter this week recognizing that they have attended. If they still refuse to sign, do not be offended. Proceed with your friendliness and the information you think they may need for the service or class being attended.

After the newcomers have signed the register, read the entries, making sure that all information is clear and complete. If a signed name is difficult to decipher, ask for the spelling. If it is pronounced differently than it is spelled, make a phonetic spelling of it on a separate paper. If a visitor has an out-of-town address, it is often appropriate to ask if he has friends or relatives who attend your church. This information is often helpful to the pastor, and it should be included on his visitors' list.

After the visitors have signed the register, give them a class and/or church brochure, a map of your facilities, and direct the visitors to the host/hostess who will assign them to an escort. If you do not use a host/hostess, assign the visitors directly to an escort.

When the visitor traffic slows, type or clearly print a list of the visitors, including:

Visitor's Name (Phonetic spelling of name if necessary)

Address

Phone

Invited by or Relatives of:

Be concise in your printing or typing, trying to limit your entries to as few pages as possible (preferably half-sheets or index cards). Make one copy for the head usher to give to the pastor, a second copy to remain at the Welcome Center, and a third copy for the church secretary.

Welcome Center Host/Hostess

The host/hostess should give the newcomers a visitor I.D. gift, preferably something that can be worn so that the congregation can easily recognize the visitors. (See Appendix C for suggestions.)

Assist the visitors with registration at the Welcome Center if necessary. Give the newcomers visitor's cards (see Appendix C for suggestions), one for each individual class to be attended. If time permits, you may want to assist them with completing these. Get acquainted, finding out the ages of the children and what classes they will attend. If your church has several adult classes that offer a variety of lesson topics, keep abreast of these changes so that you can adequately inform the newcomers. It is helpful to the regular attenders as well as the newcomers if your Christian Life and Sunday School Board or Church School Department can print a quarterly list of the classes offered, the topics being taught, the names of the teachers, and where the classes will meet.

After looking at the list made available to them, ask the adults if they have a preference of classes. If not, make a momentary evaluation and match the newcomers to the personality of the class where you feel that they would be most comfortable. Ask if they feel comfortable with your suggestion. If they do, proceed. Suggest that they try other classes in future Sundays if they so desire.

Suggest to the family that they designate a place to meet following Sunday School or worship. Suggest the Welcome Center or other area if they seem confused. Be sure to clarify whether or not the children will attend children's church and if they should meet following Sunday School or following the worship service. You may also suggest to the newcomers that they use the main sanctuary door to exit today so that you can have the opportunity to introduce them to the pastor.

Escort Greeter

An escort greeter should very briefly get acquainted with the visitors and promote friendly conversation as he escorts the visitors to a class or the sanctuary. If you see another escort ready to leave for a class, share responsibilities, one taking the children, and the other taking the adults. Flow with what feels comfortable. It is sometimes advantageous even to utilize nearby help, such as a teen or adult who you know is headed where a newcomer needs to go. Do this with discretion, however, only with someone who you know will make them feel comfortable in the class. Always say, "Would you show (give name of person) to your class and make sure that they meet your class greeter or teacher. Thanks!"

If the family has a baby, it is usually best to give the parents the option of taking the child to class with them or leaving him in the nursery. Assure them that you have an adequately staffed nursery for all the services. If they choose to use the nursery, escort them there and introduce them to the workers. Wait while registering procedures are completed. If they choose not to use the nursery, suggest showing them the nursery anyway, just in case they choose to use it during future services or even later that day.

When you arrive at the class, introduce the visitors to the class greeter. At this time you may return to the Welcome Center or your auxiliary entrance to escort others. Approximately 10 minutes after class starting time, you may go to your own Sunday School class. In fact, you are strongly encouraged to attend a class. The visitors need to know that you believe in Sunday School, too.

Sanctuary Door Greeters/Ushers

A sanctuary door greeter may also serve as an usher. Only a friendly greeting is necessary; conversation is discouraged. Your quiet enthusiasm prior to a service will help set the mood for worship. Your genuine friendliness following a service will entice the visitor to return.

Quietly offer everyone, members and visitors alike, a choice of seats and escort them to their selection. With regulars use discretion when deciding who would appreciate an escort and who would be offended by it. Always verbally give visitors a choice of seats, recognizing them by their visitor I.D. Ask them to follow you to the place of their choice. Most visitors prefer a seat halfway or further back in the sanctuary. This position in itself offers a measure of comfort, especially if the visitors are unfamiliar with your form of worship. If the majority of the congregation is in front of the visitors, they can feel more assured that they are sitting and standing and kneeling and bowing their heads at the right times.

Whenever possible, usher newcomers to an uncrowded pew with easy access. If they must pass by someone else to get to their seat, the usher should be the one to say, "Please excuse us." Use caution in asking someone to move. They may have a justified reason for being on the aisle seat. At hearing your words, they will either choose to move over or should stand or move to allow the visitors to get by them.

Larger churches will be able to keep the flow of people smoother if a crew of greeters will stand outside of the sanctuary door to welcome and distribute bulletins. Another crew should remain just inside the sanctuary doors to escort people to their seats. Both sets of greeters should cover all entrances into the sanctuary. If your sanctuary is somewhat full and people are still arriving, use one usher per aisle to scan the crowd for empty seats. They can make signals to alert the ushers who are seating people. Never seat anyone during prayer, a special song, reading of Scripture, or the sermon.

In both small and large churches, the quiet atmosphere of worship is demonstrated by the sanctuary door greeters and is best maintained when the sanctuary doors are kept closed. Foyer noise infiltrating a sanctuary destroys the worshipful attitude set by the greeters and the organist. Open the doors only when someone is ready to enter. This simple procedure should say, "Noisy fellowship takes place in the foyer, quiet preparation for worship is in progress in the sanctuary."

If you notice excessive fanning or reaching for wraps, suggest a temperature change to the head usher, but never change it yourself.

Know the location of rest rooms, nursery, fire exits, storm shelter areas, and first aid supplies and equipment. Of course, it is ideal if a greeter or usher has had C.P.R. training and can assist in an emergency, but if not, know who in your congregation is a doctor, who is a nurse, or who has had C.P.R. training. Make sure that the numbers for fire, police, and ambulance are easily accessible in case of an emergency.

Most churches ask the ushers who receive the offering to count attendance in their duty area and report it to the head usher. Your head usher will inform you of the procedure for your church.

As much as is possible, help keep disturbances to a minimum. In a loving way, let children and teens know that it disturbs a service for them to go in and out. Very kindly assure them that this time is all right, but ask them to please refrain from leaving in the future if at all possible. If it is a child whose parents do not attend, suggest that he sit by a member in the back, and help him find a place. If possible, don't allow him to return to the front and cause possible disturbance. **Be firm but never harsh.** Correct the offenders with love and compassion or refrain from correcting at all.

Except for those who are assigned to police the building, greeters and ushers may sit with their families for worship following the receiving of the offering, or after their specific responsibility is completed. Greeters and ushers should never congregate during a service to chat; it undermines the effectiveness of the pastor's message and the ministry of the church. Visitors need to sense that the ushers are as anxious to worship and participate in the service as they are to usher.

Open the sanctuary doors at the close of the service when the pastor and staff begin to exit. Otherwise, the doors should be kept closed at all times to diffuse any voice noise from the foyer.

In most churches it is customary for the pastor and staff to make themselves available at the exits at the close of a service. Your pastor may also want the greeters to assist with this responsibility, especially at the exits from the sanctuary. Make a good first and last impression on your visitors: a warm greeting and a cordial farewell.

It was Easter Sunday, and my dad, the pastor, woke with a severe sore throat. Mom secured one of the associates for the pulpit. The service went well; but upon dismissal the associates, the regular greeters, and regular attenders were busy with their usual activities and forgot to staff the exit where my dad always stood.

A new Christian recognized the situation, remembering how important a farewell at the exit was to her only weeks before. Pat grabbed her husband's hand and said, "We've got to hurry to the door and invite those people back."

En route her husband, Dick, pleaded, "But, Pat, we're new too. We don't even know the difference between the new people and the regular attenders." She replied, "Just smile and say you're happy they came to worship with us today."

A tall, young soldier and his new bride received Pat's friendly request to come back and meet her pastor, but explained, "We're on our honeymoon. I'm on my way to Vietnam, and my wife will be living in Tennessee with her parents. I'm sorry, but we won't be back."

Pat wasn't easily discouraged. She continued, "If it is ever possible, please come back. We have the best pastor and the best church in all the world."

Those words kept replaying in the honeymooners' minds. At 2 A.M. on the following Sunday, the bride woke suddenly with a brainstorm. And when a bride is awake with a brainstorm, it seems only logical to wake her husband, too. Rousing him from his sleep, she said, "John, if we get up right now, we could drive to St. Louis, hear that preacher, and see if he's as good as that lady says he is. Besides, you could take a plane from St. Louis airport, and we would be together a half day longer."

More time together is always desirable to honeymooners, so off they went to St. Louis.

When my dad greeted this couple at the door, John said, "Pastor, you would never believe the circumstances that brought us here today." He shared the story about the enthusiastic young couple who had insisted that they come back.

My dad wanted to know who these members were! He began pointing out several likely candidates. No, none of them fit the description. Then the soldier spotted the couple. "There they are, sir."

Dad questioned him, "Are you sure? They're not even members yet. They're new to our congregation."

John replied, "New or not, they're the best members that you have."

John went to Vietnam and his wife, Sharon, went to Nashville. A few months later when John received news that his sister, Shirley, was getting married, he wrote her a letter encouraging her to attend the same church that he had attended on his honeymoon.

Shirley and Dennis came. They liked it. They returned and soon accepted Jesus as their Savior. Within 10 months from that Easter Sunday when an enthusiastic young couple saw the need to be at the door as a greeter, John's mother and father and two younger brothers had also begun attending, had accepted Christ, and had joined the church.

The youngest of those brothers, Don, married my sister, Sheryl, and the ministry of that Easter morning lives on in their lives and the lives of that entire family.

Class Greeter

Every Sunday School class, teens through adults, should appoint a greeter to remain just inside the class door. The escort should introduce the visitor to the class greeter and give him the visitor's card. As a class greeter you should help the visitor find a seat and use every opportunity possible to personally introduce him to the teacher and class members. If there is a social or project planned, give the visitor a personal invitation. Also ask one of the class members to escort the visitor to the sanctuary.

In the children's classes the teacher can act as a greeter. She should find out from the escort whether or not the child is expected to meet his parents following Sunday School or if he is to attend children's church. Also ask if the parent plans to pick up the child or if the child should be escorted to the Welcome Center if that is where he is to meet his family.

There was an older Jewish couple who attended my home church one Sunday morning. They gladly introduced themselves to the pastor and all the greeters. We were soon aware of the intent of their visit when they emphasized their last name and casually let us know that their son was running for state representative. We were just one of the churches on their hit list.

We could have written them off as insincere people who were using the organization of the church for personal gain. But we didn't. Our greeters welcomed them to return.

To our surprise, they began attending regularly, accepted Christ as their Savior, and began attending Sunday School.

Fifteen years later my dad was called to take part in the funeral of this Jewish man. His wife, now crippled by arthritis, was in a wheelchair. Dad knelt in front of her, asking if she remembered him. She smiled and answered, "Yes, but there is someone I remember better than you. It is your dear mother."

Grandma was in her 80s when that Jewish lady began attending her Sunday School class. Grandma was old, but not too old to be a class greeter and a caring Christian. The lady went on to say, "I knew she loved me the first Sunday I came. She offered to help answer my questions about the services and about Christianity." Her voice cracked as she continued, "People in other churches had said that they wanted us to come back, but we were sure that they just wanted our money. Your church was different. They were so genuinely friendly that we knew that they weren't afraid of our Jewish ways, and they weren't calculating how much we were worth. Your mother taught me everything I know about Jesus. She listened to me, she gave me scriptures to read, and she prayed with me. She loved me and led me to her Jesus."

Dad admits that all those years he had thought that it was

his dynamic sermons that had taught this couple, but it really was a dedicated layperson, who just happened to be his mother. Grandma was a class greeter who saw her position as ministry.

Head Usher

It is the head usher's responsibility to make sure that an adequate group of greeters and ushers are at their post every time the door of the church is opened: for all Sunday and weekday services, special services, programs, district meetings, Christian school programs, and so on.

You should appoint an assistant, with the approval of the pastor, so someone will always be in charge in your absence.

Upon arrival at each service, check the facilities for tidiness. It is always possible that someone has "dumped" since the custodian made his last inspection. Do whatever is necessary to keep the building, especially the foyers, the Welcome Center, and auxiliary desks, very attractive and free from clutter.

Keep an adequate supply of pencils, visitor's cards, visitor I.D., greeter name tags, and such at the Welcome Center. Alert the church office secretary when a new supply needs to be ordered.

Check on the overall comfort of the people: lights, sound, and temperature. Take care of it or alert the proper persons. Watch for the pastor's signals. He may ask for a change in the lights, sound, or temperature or may need an ushering crew at a moment's notice. Be ready.

If your pastor reads the list of visitors during the service, ask him when in the service he would like to receive the list. If he does not read it, ask him when and where he would like his copy delivered.

Be prayerful in your selection of ushers. Ushering is a good place for newcomers to begin serving in the church, but be cautious not to choose just anyone for this important ministry. Use only those who are willing to go through a greeter training course or read this book. Rotate the use and the position of ushers periodically so that no one owns a position. Keep a list of assignments posted in advance.

As the head usher it will also be your responsibility to either initiate or to delegate the principles given in chapters 4 and 5 for helping the newcomers feel at home within your congregation. A questionnaire regarding the newcomers' interests, given after a few weeks of regular attendance, can be helpful. (See Appendix E.) One caution: If you use the questionnaire, plan sufficient follow-up. One thing more frustrating than not being asked to participate in ministry or in a small-group fellowship is to be asked what your desires are and then have them ignored. (You will understand this position more fully after reading chapters 4 and 5.)

Meet with your ushers and devise a system that is efficient for your size of congregation so that you can have an accurate head count of each service. Many churches ask the ushers to count each row as they take the offering, then add those in the nursery and other parts of the building. Don't forget to count yourselves and those on the platform. Strive for accuracy. Report the attendance of each service to the church office secretary by placing a note in her box or on her desk.

Keep a few ushers or greeters on duty during the services for latecomers, but encourage other ushers to sit with their families. Many churches will want an usher to lock all auxiliary doors approximately 15 minutes after starting time of all evening services and programs. Some areas will also require a periodic check of the facilities, as well as the parking lot.

With the approval of the pastor, appoint a doorkeeper or assume the doorkeeper responsibilities as listed below.

Doorkeeper

The doorkeeper is to insure that the church facility is open for use a reasonable time prior to regular services and special programs and secured following the close of these. When you open the building, see that adequate lighting is on in the foyers, hallways, and whatever rooms are to be used.

Most churches will also want you to secure all entry doors except the main foyer entrance shortly after the start of all evening services.

When securing all the doors at the close of each service, also check all rooms, including rest rooms, to make sure that all lighting is off and all windows are secured. Thermostats should also be checked for proper settings.

In the winter, make arrangements with the custodian or other ushers to clear the sidewalks prior to each service.

As a doorkeeper you will be considered a part of the greeter/usher staff and will be directly responsible to the head usher or chairperson of your Greeter/Usher Committee. If you are ever unable to perform your duties, notify the chairman or head usher so that a replacement can be secured.

Summary

Whether your church is filling the position of a general practitioner or a specialist, the success of your greeting and ushering ministry will depend largely upon your determination to make it work. Your leadership will probably choose to add to and or revise these responsibilities to custom fit your local situation, so remember to be conscientious about the general principles given in this chapter, but be extremely flexible with the specifics of implementation.

A family who recently visited our church commented that they had lost count of how many people had spoken to them. It wasn't just one individual who made them feel welcome, but it was everyone in their place, fulfilling ministry in their position. Accept your greeter position, seeing each position as equally important as the other, and make that position a place of ministry.

Group Interaction

1. Briefly discuss the differences between a general practitioner and a specialist. Which role will your church probably need to assume?

2. Brainstorm about the following greeter positions and the needs of your church. Write down ideas and present them as suggestions to those in authority. Remember to remain teachable, just in case they see the situation and the needs differently than you do.

    a. How could a parking lot and/or portico greeter be effective in your local church?

    b. What entrances does your church need to staff with greeters? Approximately how many at each?

    c. Discuss the positions of door greeter, Welcome Center secretary, Welcome Center host/hostess, escorts, and the sanctuary door greeter/usher, and what your needs are for these positions.

    d. Where is the most accessible place for your Welcome Center? Should the Welcome Center be a desk, a table, or should you consider building one? (See Appendix B for sketches and suggestions.)

    e. How could Sunday School class greeters make your greeting ministry more effective?

3. After learning more about the ministry as well as the expectations of each position, complete the greeter assignment form in Appendix D or one that your leadership has compiled for you. Do not be so humble that you fail to show a preference for a certain position. But also don't be so proud that you are

willing to take only the high-exposure jobs. Pray and ask God where He wants to use you. Return this form to your head usher or pastor.

4. Review the Time Line Checklist in Appendix A. At this point in your planning you need to make some definite decisions on the type of name tags you will use for your greeters and ushers, the type of visitor I.D., and the type of cards and/or register that you will use. Make some proposals.

3

First Impressions:
Killers or Keepers

Be wise in the way you act toward outsiders; make the most of every opportunity. Let your conversation be always full of grace, seasoned with salt, so that you may know how to answer everyone (Col. 4:5-6).

* * * * *

His intent was that now, through the church, the manifold wisdom of God should be made known to the rulers and authorities in the heavenly realms (Eph. 3:10).

* * * * *

In the same way your Father in heaven is not willing that any of these little ones should be lost (Matt. 18:14).

* * * * *

The King will reply, "I tell you the truth, whatever you did for one of the least of these brothers of mine, you did for me" (Matt. 25:40).

* * * * *

For out of the overflow of the heart the mouth speaks (Matt. 12:34).

Occasionally your congregation will be blessed with new-comers who have chosen to try your church because of the name on the outside sign. They are familiar with your doctrine, and they know what they want when they enter your doors. A grouchy greeter or an unthoughtful usher who escorts them and their two-year-old to the front seat is not likely to deter them. Such newcomers, though easy bait, are a rarity.

Most of the newcomers who enter our church doors know very little about our doctrine. They come looking for a group of people with whom they will feel comfortable. They hope that they will not find the doctrine to be contrary with their established beliefs, but that consideration is usually secondary.

Because most newcomers come in search of "the right group of people," it is extremely important that we discuss a few guidelines that will heighten your chances of favorably impressing the newcomers with yourself. Realizing that you may be directly responsible for people deciding to return or not to return to your church is a weighty responsibility, but we must reckon with the fact that if we offend the newcomers, our church may never have a chance to minister to them.

We might feel frustrated by 1 Sam. 16:7, which reminds us that man looks on the outward appearance but God looks on the heart. At times we wish that our hearts were all that counted, that personality flaws and idiosyncrasies didn't matter to people, that they would just see our hearts. Nevertheless, since newcomers do not have God's perspective but rather look "at the outward appearance," we must be concerned with what they see and feel when they are with us.

Recently I was employed by a temporary job placement service. I realized that the prospective employer was interested in more than just office skills when I was told to come to the interview dressed as if I were going to an office for an assignment. At the close of the interview, these suspicions were confirmed when they informed me that I had been graded not only on my office skills but also on my appearance and mannerisms: the way I dressed, the way I handled myself, my smile, and my style.

Whether we like it or not, people do watch us and analyze us. They will watch you as a greeter and will analyze your church by the impressions you give them.

The following guidelines are simple; some are obvious, others are often overlooked. Read them carefully and evaluate your greeting skills, not from your perspective or even God's perspective, but from the perspective of newcomers.

1. Arrive Early

Since visitors almost always arrive early, it is vital that greeters arrive earlier. What is earlier? Your earlier will be determined by your community's personality: early bird fellowshipers or slide-in-the-door-just-under-the-wire roadrunners. Determine the personality of your community, then schedule greeters to be in their positions prior to the first arrival. It is safe to estimate 20-30 minutes prior to Sunday School, worship, and other regularly scheduled services, and 45-60 minutes for special services such as programs and concerts.

2. Report In

As soon as you arrive, report to the secretary at the Welcome Center. Pick up your name tag and/or greeter I.D., and check the supplies that you may need according to your position. At the close of each service, return your name tag, greeter I.D., and all excess supplies to the Welcome Center. Wearing a name tag not only helps the newcomers to learn your name, but the mere presence of the name tag identifies you as someone who can help them if they have a question.

3. Check Your Appearance

Your appearance often will make a lasting first impression on a newcomer. Present your church as a place where holiness standards are regarded. Avoid extravagances in makeup, accessories, and styles. Most churches prefer that men wear a suit and tie and that ladies wear a suit or dress. Some churches prefer a more casual appearance, however, for midweek services. Allow your pastor to help you set these guidelines to fit your congregation.

The newcomers may not notice that you took special care to have neatly groomed hair, clean nails, and fresh breath, but they will be unfavorably impressed by the lack of such. It's probably best to refrain from chewing gum to freshen your breath, since chewing is often offensive to some people.

4. Anticipate the Newcomers

It is easy to become involved in conversation with a fellow greeter or friend and miss the newcomers. Watch for the newcomers and keep your conversations with friends to a minimum.

When people enter the door whom you do not recognize, approach them by saying, "We're glad to have you here today. I don't recall meeting you before. Is this your first visit to our church?" If they answer "Yes," proceed with *a*; if they say, "No," proceed with *b*.

   a. "I am (give your name), and what is your name?" Listen intently as they give their name. (See Guideline 5.) "So glad to meet you. If you'll step to the Welcome Center, they will help you register and will find someone to direct you to your class (or the sanctuary)."

If your church does not use a hostess/host at the Welcome Center, then you will need to make a brief acquaintance before you have them sign the register or visitor's card.

   b. "I am (give your name), and please remind me of your

name." If it seems appropriate, perhaps you could ask, "Have you attended some of our special services or do you attend here regularly?" Make the conversation brief, but long enough so that they feel that you are sincerely wanting to recognize them the next time that they come.

Most small churches, and even some larger churches, do not have visitors every Sunday, so it is easy to give up on a greeting ministry. You may wait by the door for weeks just to welcome one visitor, but don't give up. Keep anticipating the newcomer. Your weeks of waiting will be rewarded when that newcomer is impressed by your friendliness and is compelled to come again because of your warmth.

5. Develop Your Skill of Remembering Names

Although it is not mandatory for a greeter to be able to remember names, it is certainly helpful. Even though you may be convinced that you do not have the gift of remembering names, perhaps these suggestions can improve what skills you have.

a. Listen intently. Often people have been introduced to me, and by the time they were a few steps away, I realized that I couldn't recall their name. Why? I wasn't listening intently. I may have even repeated their name, but my mind was wandering and did not retain it. To remember a name, you must consciously listen with your ears and your mind.

b. Repeat the name immediately to make sure that you have heard it correctly. Ask for the spelling, if necessary, to aid in remembering the pronunciation of the name.

c. If possible, make some kind of association with their name: a word that rhymes, someone they look like, a relative by that name, or the uniqueness of the name. A warning: Use caution in relaying your association to the visitors. You may be proud of your ingenious clue to remembering, but they may be offended by it.

d. At the close of the conversation repeat their name again, for their benefit and yours.

e. If possible, introduce them to someone immediately to have the opportunity to use their name. If that is not possible, use their name in conversation with someone that day to keep it fresh in your memory.

f. Write the name down as soon as possible. Review it often until you can recall it easily. It is worth your effort to consciously try to develop your skill of remembering names, for nothing satisfies the ego need and the need of belonging quite like having someone remember your name.

6. Welcome Everyone

Not only do the newcomers need your consistency at your place of duty, but also the regular attenders need a friendly greeting. They need to be asked occasionally how they are doing. The attention you give your regular attenders when noticing their return after a vacation or hospital stay will please them. A greeter can often sense when a regular attender is particularly discouraged and needs prayer and encouragement. Remember that as a greeter you represent the friendliness and caring attitude of Christ and your entire church.

Your greeting should also include the children. I recently heard the account of a very sad little girl who threw herself across the bed and sobbed when she got home from visiting her granny's church. In bewilderment her grandmother asked, "What is wrong?" Between her sobs the little girl exclaimed, "No one likes me at your church. Everyone said hi to you and shook your hand, but nobody said hi or shook my hand!" Children need to be welcomed, too.

Although everyone should be greeted with a cheery welcome and warm smile, a handshake is not always necessary. Especially be considerate of young parents with arms full of children and their accessories. I have seen people nearly drop their children as they tried to reach for the extended hand of a well-meaning greeter. Assist everyone's entry, but don't overwhelm them and cause a disaster.

Men should especially be cautious to use discretion in shaking a woman's hand. It is usually acceptable only to shake a woman's hand if she extends hers to you.

7. Check Your Handshake

Even your handshake has a personality and makes an impression on those you greet. What kind of handshake do you have?

Do you remember the handshake of someone you weren't sure was attached to their hand? You knew that there was a body standing before you, but their life was not in their hand. It felt like a fish, you thought. Oh, how you wished they would grip just a little so the funny chill going down your spine would quit.

And then there were those whose fighter grip left you flexing your knuckles as you walked away. Recalling their intense strength made you vow to avoid their handshake in the future if at all possible. At least if you couldn't avoid it, you would try holding your breath during the ordeal in hopes it would lessen the pain.

The forever handshake could win a Boston marathon. Your elbow throbbed, and you feared a disjointed arm socket as the shake shook forever. While the shaker kept rhythm with his conversation, your mind wandered, wondering if this shaking would ever come to an end.

Poor, frightened handshake happened so fast. You feared that you had done something to offend him.

There are the "fish," the "fighters," the "forevers," and the "frightened," but people want a "friend." They need a handshake that is firm but painless, warm but not gushy, enthusiastic but not tiring.

Since you probably don't make a practice of shaking your own hand, ask a close friend to candidly evaluate your handshake and help you make corrections if necessary.

8. Be Space Conscious

Everyone has a territorial perimeter. If you go beyond that perimeter without permission, people feel uneasy. Most people feel that a comfortable speaking distance is 2½ to 3 feet. Farther than 3 feet, they may feel that you are aloof. Closer than 2½ feet, they may feel suffocated by you.

Guarding a person's territorial perimeter is often an area where we are not conscious of our own habits. For clues to your habits, watch visitors' body language. Especially be conscious of being too close. If people move back a step while you are talking, don't move toward them. They are probably letting you know that you were too close. Also refrain from hugs and other bodily contact or body language that might invade the visitors' territorial perimeters.

9. Be Enthusiastic

Body language often says more than our words. Speak, act, and be enthusiastic. You may have had a bad morning, you're fighting a horrible headache, and your arthritis causes you to cringe every time someone shakes your hand, but don't give a hint of discomfort or the blahs to those you greet. Be excited about your personal walk with Christ. Be excited about your Sunday School class and what it is helping you to learn from God's Word. Be excited about the programs that your church offers to meet the varied needs of your family. (It may not be doing everything you wish it would, but concentrate on the positive things.) Be excited about your pastor and staff and their desire to care for their congregation. Although you will rarely have a chance to verbally express your enthusiasm, your body language will tell everyone what's in your heart. Your spirit will be contagious; let it be a Christ-filled spirit of enthusiasm.

Summary

Your pews may not be padded, and your choir may not have perfect pitch, but visitors will usually overlook your structural flaws if they are favorably impressed with you as a greeter when they enter your church. Newcomers are most impressed by your friendliness. To be an effective greeter for your church, you should add to these guidelines and your friendliness the attitudes of teachability, commitment, and prayerfulness.

As a teachable greeter you will be willing to listen to the leadership within your church and willing to make changes as time and situations demand. Every church situation is unique, and every community responsive to different methods. Time and social changes also alter the effectiveness of our methods. A teachable person will not resist change but will eagerly learn from it.

For the greeting ministry to be most effective in your church, it must be organized; and a teachable greeter will be willing to fit within that organization whether it is elaborate or minimal. If your church offers training sessions, it will be beneficial for you to attend them, even though you have held a greeting position for years. To be the most effective, learn to work as a team, not as an individual.

In accepting a greeting position, you will make a commitment to regular attendance. To visitors who return, your presence will speak of security and familiarity. The more services you miss, the less effective you will be in recognizing the visitors, and the less confidence you will have in greeting those who are returning for the second or third time.

If you must be absent, you should contact your head usher or other designated leadership as soon as possible so that a replacement can be obtained. Never leave your post unattended. A visitor may need someone in that place on that day.

Lastly, a greeter who prays to be used of God is invaluable to the church and the Kingdom. As you open your heart to the Holy Spirit's leadership, He can direct your every word and action. You can be sensitive to those who are hurting. You can give help to those who need special attention. You can smile, shake hands, get acquainted; see yourself as being Christ to those you meet. "Be wise in the way you act toward outsiders; make the most of every opportunity" (Col. 4:5).

Group Interaction

1. Discuss the personality of your community and congregation and set some guidelines for greeter arrival times for each of your services and programs.

2. Discuss the importance of a neat appearance. Leave the decision of specific guidelines, however, to your pastor.

3. Role-play in order to practice welcoming a visitor. Introduce three or more of the class by giving them fictitious names. See how many can recall their names.

4. Review the five kinds of handshakes. Stand and take a few minutes to shake hands with each other, being conscious of your handshake personality and the corrections that might need to be made.

5. Can you still recall the fictitious names given in exercise 3?

6. What are some of the things within your life and the life of your church that give you reason to be enthusiastic?

4

By All Means Keep Some

Therefore encourage one another and build each other up, just as in fact you are doing (1 Thess. 5:11).

* * * * *

"As excellent Christians, our primary goal in life must be to attract and disciple outsiders into our nourishing fellowship. That is why we are servants, live a simplified lifestyle, and are filled with the Holy Spirit (see Acts 1:8). As God guides us in weaving a 'love web' around their hearts, our own love becomes increasingly more excellent.

"Giving spiritual birth to one of his creation, for whom his only Son died, transcends the joy of giving biological birth. Or it should. It is like saying to someone lost in sin: 'Welcome to an eternity of joy. Meet the greatest people in the world, the *koinonia*—the fellowship of believers—who are filled with God's own Spirit!'"[1]

* * * * *

She did what she could (Mark 14:8).

---

1. Jon Johnston, *Christian Excellence: Alternative to Success* (Kansas City: Nazarene Publishing House, 1985), 128.

If we are going to have an opportunity to minister to the newcomer, we must keep him returning Sunday after Sunday. Even though he may have been impressed by your first royal welcome, will he continue to attend the services if he does not still feel welcome when he becomes a familiar face to the greeters?

The visitor who has bravely chosen to overcome his fears and try your church has probably come for two reasons: (1) He desires to have his spiritual hunger satisfied, and (2) he needs the fellowship and support of Christian friends. Although we agree that the greatest need is the spiritual need, seldom will a visitor remain long enough to have his spiritual needs met unless we first meet his fellowship needs.

Convinced then that your church can meet the spiritual needs of your community if given the opportunity, your primary goal as a greeter is to make newcomers feel so welcome that they will return regularly to listen to the preached Word by your pastor, study the Bible with a Sunday School class, and eventually become integrated into the other ministries of the church.

When do newcomers reach the point of feeling at home within the body of the church? When they recognize and are recognized by a significant majority, and when they are on a first-name basis with a significant minority of the congregation. This is where the small church and the large church differ. In a small church, a newcomer will need to be recognized by a larger majority than in a large church. In the larger church, a newcomer usually agrees that it is nigh to impossible to recognize, and be recognized by, everyone within the congregation. He agrees that being recognized by 50 percent, or even less, of the congregation is "feeling at home." In a smaller church, however, his expectations of the majority are much greater. Therefore, the small church needs to include everyone, or almost everyone, in their smiling majority.

While the warm feeling from a majority is craved, intimacy with a minority is almost mandatory within the large and the small church. I am not promoting the need to match ardent friends, for many people do not necessarily want that. What they need, however, is a small group of friends, 2-30, with whom they can share their joys: the birth of a child, moving into a new home, a promotion at work, and the excitement of their retirement. They also need that small group with whom they can share their sorrows: the death of a loved one, a severe illness that demands gifts of casseroles and baby-sitting, the loss of a job, or a forced retirement.

Before I expound on some of the organized fellowships that you can use to create these bonds and meet these needs (see chapter 5), let's look at some of the ministries perhaps already available within your church that could meet these needs. These ministries just need someone who will catch the burden of ministry within that program and will allow the head usher, a greeter, or whoever the head usher has appointed, to funnel the newcomers into the group that fits them. (See chapter 2—Head Usher; also Appendix E.) A greeter or usher who is already active in the suggested ministry is the best source for integrating the newcomers.

Although all churches will not likely have all of these ministries available, review the one or two that you do have, and discover how to use the ministry already available within that activity.

The Choir

We let anyone sing in our choir who thinks that he can make a joyful noise. Occasionally we have discovered that some additions are not harmonious, but we have decided that if the addition has given a newcomer a place to serve and belong, it's worth the occasional sour notes. I realize that some churches, because of limited space in their choir loft, must be selective with their choir. In either situation, whether you have the open or selective policy, keep your focus on ministry within your choir.

Our home mission church had a choir. Every year no matter how humble our efforts, we presented a Christmas and Easter cantata. It seemed a bit silly the first year when nearly the entire congregation came to the platform, but the few who remained in the pews enjoyed our efforts, and each year our audience grew. Cantatas went well because it was easier to get a commitment for only eight weeks of practice, rather than a commitment for once a week for the rest of their lives.

For three years we enjoyed the cantatas but struggled for a weekly choir. We didn't sing every Sunday, because we didn't practice every Wednesday night. For some reason it seemed senseless for the pianist to accompany and the director to lead a duet. My husband had vision nonetheless. He encouraged the few choir members to keep looking for talent, believing that someday we would have a choir who would sing every Sunday.

One of our faithful altos took my husband's talent search suggestion seriously. One Wednesday night Linda brought her neighbor, Connie. She was not a Christian and had never been in a Protestant church before, but she did love music and enjoyed singing.

Connie attended weeks of practices, with the side benefit of midweek service, long before she came to sing in a Sunday worship service. Although our style of worship was strange to her and our songs were new, the songs became more than a way to use her beautiful voice; they became messages from God to her heart.

Because Connie's husband wanted to hear her sing, he also began attending worship services. It wasn't long until Ed's heart was also touched by the messages of the songs and the love of the people. The church, their neighbors, and the choir continued to nurture this couple until they both accepted the Lord Jesus as their personal Savior, were baptized, joined the church, and became spiritual pillars within the church.

Connie's attendance, and the prospect of the choir actually being a ministry (more than just in the Sunday morning service), encouraged others to be committed to the choir, and at last we had a sanctuary choir to sing every Sunday morning. The choir was the significant few who saw it as their ministry to love Connie and Ed into the Kingdom.

Could some of your newcomers be loved by a choir?

Sports

We moved to a church a few years ago where the softball league was a constant source of contention within the church. Being newcomers ourselves, it was easy to stand back with a nonpartisan attitude to analyze the situation. Side A said, "We need the physical activity, and we want our church to endorse it." ("And help a little financially, too"—now that's where the problem was.) Side B said, "We have more important things to do with our time and our money. We should be out winning the lost instead of hitting a ball around a field."

My wise husband devised a compromise: The activity of sports would be used as an avenue of ministry. We would win the lost through the ball games, not instead of them.

The existing ball team selected a committee to set some policy statements and to list some strategies for ministry. One of the most effective rules was that in order to play, a team member would have to attend at least one of the church services each week.

Sides A and B were reluctantly but successfully united as we had a Sunday evening dedication and sending service for our ball team. The team members prayed sincerely that God would use their team for the purpose of ministry. Their prayers have been honored. Numerous families have found a place to belong, have found a significant few to love them, and have been ministered to by the ball team. The ball team was the significant minority that gave these families a sense of belonging.

So many have been drawn to the Lord and to the church through the softball team that we now have a men's competitive team, a men's fun team, a father-son team, a ladies team, besides basketball teams and golf leagues. These teams have not been organized to entertain ourselves but rather to make additional places for the newcomer to be loved by a significant few.

Could some of your newcomers be loved by a sports team?

Women's Ministries

The women of some churches thrive on monthly fellowship nights. That's great if yours does, but ours did not. The older ladies were afraid to drive at night, the younger ladies couldn't find sitters, and the middle-aged ladies felt the need to remain at home to comfort their husbands who were going through mid-life crisis.

What has worked, however, is a 10- to 12-week session each Thursday morning, September through November and another 10- to 12-week session each Thursday morning, February through May. Just like the fellowship nights held by many churches, our morning sessions meet our fellowship need, but they also have provided a chance for in-depth spiritual growth and outreach.

Not only have these morning sessions provided a place for often-neglected people to serve, but also they have provided a protected group where needs can be shared and burdens lifted. Best of all, they have provided a small group where newcomers to our congregation can feel at home. There have been numerous ladies who have been loved to Jesus and the church because of women's ministries.

We have numerous other activities throughout the year, both daytime and evening, that are sponsored by the women's ministries, but we have ceased planning activities to just entertain ourselves. Whatever we do, we do it with ministry to the newcomer in mind.

Could some of your newcomers be loved by a women's ministries group?

Men's Prayer Fellowship

My husband and 5 to 25 other men rise every Tuesday and Thursday morning early enough to attend 6:30 prayer meeting before going to work. I probably am a distant cousin of Job's wife, for I have often pleaded with my husband to disband with the early prayer meeting, or at least have it only once a week. I feel so sorry for him when he gets so little sleep, but for five years nothing has persuaded him to quit. Why? There is a fellowship need met within that small group that nothing else can fulfill. The average attendance is only 5 to 10, but about 25 men feel that the Men's Prayer Fellowship is their "significant few" to whom they can go when they have a need. The group has not become an elite clique but rather seeks to include and minister to the newcomer. Several new men to our congregation have found their sense of belonging because of this ministry.

As my husband watches the spiritual growth within this group and also senses the newcomers need for belonging to such a group, he sees God at work, answering their prayers, and he continues to say, "We need it." And I continue to wake him even when I feel that his body needs the sleep.

Could some of your newcomers be loved by a prayer fellowship?

Sunday School Classes

A Sunday School class should be a special haven within

the church, a place of comfort for the newcomer as well as the members. A newcomer feels most at ease in a class where the teacher never calls on a class member to read or pray spontaneously. To those of us who are used to this method, it may be difficult to understand the newcomers fear, but how does he know that he won't be next on the hit list?

A newcomer also needs a Sunday School class that will include him in preclass and after-class conversation. I've been in some classes that provided comfort only for the members. They were such a close-knit group that a newcomer could never feel like he belonged. A Sunday School class needs to feel close to one another, but they also always need to remain open to enlarge their circle of friendships to include the newcomer.

Socials are an excellent opportunity to include the newcomer. I've heard some narrow-minded people say, "The only time that couple ever shows up is when we offer free food." I say, "Then for Christ's sake, and the sake of their salvation, offer free food as often as possible."

There is a family in our church today because of invitations to some Sunday School class socials. They only attended our church once and never even came to our Sunday School. I admit that I haven't always felt prodded to do this, but for one year I sent this couple an invitation to all of our class socials with a personal note attached.

One day when their world seemingly crashed in around them, it was the church with the Sunday School class who cared where they went for help. Today they are consistent attenders and are the ones planning the socials and extending the invitations to the newcomers.

A Sunday School class can also provide the prayer support that people need. Not all requests are appropriate from the pulpit. I didn't want my sister-in-law's pregnancy problems spelled out from the pulpit, but I depended on the specific prayers of my Sunday School class for that critical situation. The newcomer also needs that prayer support and feels more comfortable to share a prayer need with a class rather than an entire congregation.

Especially within the large church, a Sunday School class can meet the newcomer's need of knowing a "significant few" within the church. A newcomer who could easily become lost in the crowd of a large congregation can be ministered to by a Sunday School class. A class can also better monitor the newcomer's attendance for the purpose of sensing needs, and they can become more personally acquainted for the purpose of meeting those needs.

Could some of your newcomers be loved by a Sunday School class?

Summary

Your church may offer golf leagues, craft classes, ball teams, a motorcycle club, a dinner club, a sewing circle or quilting bee, a Mothers' Day Out or a Mothers' Club, a weekly in-home Bible study, an antique car club, Caravan, youth ministries, and Vacation Bible School. Whatever programs you have or want to begin, utilize these to minister to and include the newcomers. Make ministry within these groups your number one priority. As soon as you discover the newcomers' hobbies or talents, integrate them into a group within the church who shares those same interests, who can be their "significant minority," who will help them feel at home within your church. As a greeter/usher, ask your head usher or pastor how you can best channel the newcomers into the existing small-group ministries within your church.

Group Interaction

1. On a chalkboard or newsprint, list all of the existing pro-

grams within your local church. Now review the list, discussing how each can be expanded to integrate the newcomer into your church family and minister more effectively.

2. Determine whether or not you will need an Interest Questionnaire. (See Appendix E.) If so, who will design it to fit your church's needs, who will distribute it, and how often should it be distributed?

3. If the head usher desires assistance, while looking at the ministries listed in exercise 1, make suggestions of possible contact people (greeters/ushers or otherwise) who would be the liaison between the head usher and the ministries for the purpose of integrating the newcomers into their areas of interest.

4. Is there a new ministry that you would like to consider beginning in your church? List only visions that you are willing to support with your energies in planning and implementing. No fair having a vision for someone else. Remember, your dreams will be only suggestions to be given to these existing ministries. They may have committees and ideas of their own. Respect them. It would be exciting, however, if your pastor feels that it would be advantageous, to call a meeting of the directors of each of these ministries to meet with your greeting committee to dream together about ministry to the newcomer.

5. Brochures and maps are appreciated by the newcomer. What are your needs and plans for this? Discuss the need of a map of your facilities, either a stationary map or a hand-out map. Discuss the need of a brochure to list Sunday School classes available and/or the ministries available within your church.

5

Fragile: Handle with Fellowship

Watch out that you do not lose what you have worked for, but that you may be rewarded fully. Anyone who runs ahead and does not continue in the teaching of Christ does not have God; whoever continues in the teaching has both the Father and the Son (2 John 8-9).

You did not choose me, but I chose you . . . to go and bear fruit—fruit that will last. Then the Father will give you whatever you ask in my name (John 15:16).

* * * * *

Offer hospitality to one another without grumbling. Each one should use whatever gift he has received to serve others, faithfully administering God's grace in its various forms (1 Pet. 4:9-10).

* * * * *

Therefore go and make disciples of all nations, baptizing them in the name of the Father and of the Son and of the Holy Spirit, and teaching them to obey everything I have commanded you. And surely I am with you always, to the very end of the age (Matt. 28:19-20).

A few years ago at a Church Schools Convention, we sat for perhaps 30 minutes viewing slides of a tree farm and nursery. We were educated about planting, watering, feeding, and caring for trees. About 20 minutes into this presentation I thought, This is really wonderful to have the chance to learn about trees, but we're at a Church Schools Convention. Why are they wasting our time on tree education?

We soon learned that it was not time wasted, for we learned an analogy that would prod my Christianity for years to come. When we think of a tree, we think of stability, usefulness, and grandeur. But a sapling does not have those qualities. If a newly planted tree does not have the protection of a nursery, its survival rate is very slim. It must remain in the protection of a nursery for two years before it can safely be transplanted to the tree farm. Even then, the saplings are tenderly watched. If they survive the first growing season on the farm, then the growers are assured that they will survive most anything in your yard or mine. Think about it—it takes three years to get a tree ready to stand on its own.

Perhaps we need to view our newcomers as seeds, newly planted. We need to surround them with love and fellowship until they have weathered enough growing seasons to be fully integrated into the mainstream of our church. They need the care of a spiritual nursery until they are stable enough to produce on their own.

Although it is possible that the list of existing ministries within your church is very limited, you can still attract the newcomer. You may have only one adult class and no extras, but you can offer the newcomer fellowship.

Not even the larger church will probably use all of the following suggested ministries simultaneously; so no matter what size your church is, read this chapter prayerfully and consider how at least one of these fellowship ministries could effectively help your church.

Visitation

I have been exposed to many varied visitation programs in the churches where I grew up and where my husband has pastored. I remember the good old days when my mother would cook supper for about 50 people every Wednesday night. Many came straight from work and met their families at the church. After a quick meal, the children would stay with a sitter while the teens and adults went calling for one hour prior to the midweek service. The results were rewarding, and the children of those who attended those visitation suppers had such pleasant memories of visitation night that they grew up not having the fear of visiting in the home of the newcomer.

My brother's church has a revised version of our memorable visitation supper that has been adapted for this hurried, overcommitted generation. Their visitation program is active only during "soup weather": fall and early spring. The ladies take turns bringing enough of their favorite soup to feed the visitation crew, and someone else supplies the bread and beverage.

This soup supper visitation program has both simplicity and brevity in its favor. So many visitation programs fail because they are too complex, and the workers become overwhelmed and overcommitted.

Two of the churches we have pastored have tried the pegboard method. Visitation secretaries prepare the cards of absentees and visitors and place them on the hooks to be picked up by the visitation crew. One church had a designated calling night, and the other let the volunteers make their calls whenever they could. Both had periodic success.

Almost all visitation programs, however, can be successful if your expectations are not too high. If your church has only one couple who feels that their ministry is to call on the newcomers, then thank God for one couple. If your church can support a highly organized visitation program, then work it. Keep in mind, though, that few programs keep their vitality and effectiveness from one generation, or even year, to another. They periodically need revisions or even rests.

During the time of revision or rest, don't give in to failure. The newcomers who enter your doors need a call from one of your laypersons soon after their visit to your church. Your method of accomplishing that is unimportant; just see that it gets done. Never cease reaching out by way of in-home visitation because of repeated program failures. Revise your program, simplify your program, but keep reaching out to say, "Our church can be your home."

Let your head usher or pastor know if you would like to be involved in visitation.

Fellowship Dinners

There is nothing like breaking bread together for breaking down the barriers to communication. You may have sat only a pew away from someone for years, but if you have not eaten with them, you probably do not really know them.

My husband's first place of ministry was as a minister of youth at my home church. My dad was the senior pastor of this church of 500 attenders but had known the days of a small church, too. He began that church with only 2 members and 2 other attenders: my mother, a longtime friend, my baby brother, and me. He really knew what small was. He also knew that the large church had to keep a semblance of the small-church atmosphere, or it would lose its warmth and friendliness, especially to the newcomer.

To maintain this friendly atmosphere, we divided the entire church into six groups. Each group organized a setup committee and a cleanup committee. Each family within that group was asked to bring three large dishes to pass on their given Sunday: a meat or casserole dish, a vegetable or salad dish, and a dessert. The beverages and table service were provided by the church. These six groups rotated so that a fabulous meal was prepared every Sunday.

Each Sunday morning when the newcomers were greeted, they were informed that dinner was already prepared for them in the fellowship hall, and we would like for them to share a time of fellowship with us following the service. Most everyone accepted our invitation. They were also encouraged to share dinner with us, on us, for the next five weeks so that they could meet the other five-sixths of our congregation. On the seventh week they would be assigned to a group and would become a part of this ministry to other newcomers if they wished.

No wonder the community said that we lived up to our slogan, "The End of Your Search for a Friendly Church."

When my husband and I began our ministry in a home mission church, we wanted a similar ministry for our small congregation. Only one problem! If we divided our congregation into six groups, there would be one Sunday without a family. We revised the program to meet our small church's needs.

For our small church we designated the first Sunday of each month as Fellowship Sunday. When a newcomer was greeted, they were informed that a special dinner in their honor would be held on the first Sunday of the month. The pastoral letter that followed their visit also contained an invitation to this dinner. Numerous families were added to our congregation because of the friendship and food that was offered on those Fellowship Sundays.

Fellowship Nights

If you do not have a fellowship hall adequate for dinners, perhaps your church would like the Fellowship Night. The first thing to do is to check your church calendar for a Sunday evening that would not usually conflict with after-church teen activities and so on. Let's say that you choose the third Sunday night of each month. Begin on the fourth Sunday advertising next month's Fellowship Night. Each time you advertise, reinforce the three simple rules: (1) Everyone is to invite someone to their home for fellowship following the evening service (and no fair waiting to be invited). (2) You must invite someone who has never before been in your home for fellowship. (3) Keep the refreshments simple. Do not try to impress each other with your food or your homes. Just enjoy each other.

This Fellowship Night not only gives the newcomers a chance to be in the homes of your congregation, but it stimulates the entire body to get to know one another better! This can be the impetus that many need to reach beyond their family or peer groups for fellowship.

Open Home Committee

The Open Home Committee may be comprised of only one or several who agree to open their homes to any newcomer. They can open their homes especially on Fellowship Nights for the newcomers who have not received an invitation by the Sunday morning of the Fellowship Night, or they can use any weeknight or Sunday of their choice for this ministry.

Those on the Open Home Committee often will have the opportunity to suggest programs and ministries within the church where the newcomer may desire to become involved. Because of the friendship established through the in-home fellowship, it will also become natural for the members of the Open Home Committee to introduce the newcomer to new friends at church. The Open Home Committee can also become an unofficial prayer support group who prays for the newcomers and periodically checks on them until they are assured that they have found sufficient friends and feel integrated into the life of the church.

In our church we have not made this committee a highly organized or highly publicized committee. We just have several families who feel that opening their home, usually for Sunday dinner, is their part in the greeting ministry. They check often with the head usher and the pastor to see who needs an invitation to their home. They minister so quietly, but we hear the results of their loving efforts as newcomers remark, "I can't believe that we have been invited into people's homes. This church is so friendly. We feel so welcome here." Only a few families have conveyed that message through a shared meal, but the entire church gets the credit and reaps the results.

Get-Acquainted Portraits

There are not too many homes in the world that have our family portrait displayed, but I guarantee you that wherever my likeness adorns the wall or piano, I feel at home there. A displayed portrait has a way of saying, "You are special to us. You belong here."

A few years ago when we were struggling with keeping our congregation aware of the newcomers after they no longer wore their visitor I.D., Richard, a professional photographer, began attending our church. Since he was also new and recognized our dilemma, he was willing to help.

We designed a Get-Acquainted Portrait Board. A lady who was gifted with crafts was asked to make a permanent board that could be displayed on a decorative easel in the foyer. After newcomers had begun to attend with some regularity, the head usher or Richard approached the newcomers and asked to schedule a portrait. These framed portraits along with a typed listing of the individual and family names was attached to the board. (See Appendix F for suggestions.) So we do not inadvertently miss anyone, occasionally we put a note in our weekly newsletter and the Sunday bulletin asking newcomers to contact the church office if they would like their portrait taken.

The Get-Acquainted Portrait Board serves three vital purposes:

1. It gives the regulars a chance to study names and faces so that they can greet the newcomers without embarrassment.

2. It also helps the newcomers recognize that they are not the only ones struggling with being new. I often see newcomers gravitate to one another after viewing the portraits, realizing that they have something in common. They begin welcoming each other.

3. Once a portrait has been displayed, there is a sense of belonging even though the newcomers have not officially become members of the congregation.

After the portrait has been displayed for several weeks, or even several months, it is given to the family as a gift from the church. (Throughout this book I have often referred to visitors as "families." Of course, a single person is also considered a "family." Treat individuals with the same interest and enthusiasm as a family.)

Conclusion

Since I was only three when Dad began his home mission church, I grew with the church. I don't remember those Sundays when Dad says he preached to five or less. My most vivid memories are from the time when the Sunday School rooms were bulging, and we were beginning Building Program No. 2. Since Dad stayed at the same church for 31 years, and since our first ministry assignment was at this church, it was easy to find my place of comfort within the church. I held the positions I liked and did the enjoyable jobs, and there were plenty of people to do all the things that "weren't within the realm of my gifts."

Perhaps the Lord thought that I needed to be taught about expanding the "realm of my gifts." When my husband announced that the Lord was leading him to pastor a church, I gave the Lord a map and showed Him the areas where I'd be willing to go, where I would be comfortable with said realm of gifts. The Lord surely has a sense of humor, for He chose a place that wasn't even on most maps—a place where I knew that I would not fit. He was asking us not only to pastor a church but also to start a church. We only had 17 prospective members, and all but 3 of them were military and weren't sure how long they'd be around. I asked my husband to check with the Lord again.

Daily the Lord received reasons why we wouldn't fit in this home mission, military situation. It was much too small. Being used to a big church with all its programs, I would probably turn inside out and burn out at an early age, trying to do everything that was necessary for ministry. Besides, since it was predominantly a military congregation, we would constantly be faced with saying "good-byes." Again, being used to a stable community, I was sure it wouldn't be feasible to adjust to constant change.

As you know, the Lord won. When we submitted to God's will, we began to feel a strange warmth for the little town of Waynesville, and we accepted this assignment sight unseen. We don't always recommend that, but in this case, the Lord probably knew that was the only way we would have accepted.

On our initial visit to Waynesville we left the interstate that wound between the foothills of the Ozark mountains. We took the business route through what was to become our hometown. We gasped as we saw bars, tattoo shops, massage parlors, and more bars, and more tattoo shops, and more massage parlors. There was only one grocery store and a True Value hardware store. How could we ever build a church in this type of community? We spent a sleepless night almost dreading Sunday morning and wondering if there was any way we could reverse our decision to move.

That next morning as we entered the tiny Seventh Day Adventist church our people had rented for Sunday services, we sensed their excitement, and some of our feelings of dread began to disappear. I was still plagued, though, with the dilemma of growing a church in this type of community. Nevertheless, by the end of the day we traveled home, assured that God would help us establish a church in Waynesville.

We moved with enthusiasm to "our mission field." After a few weeks, however, I was alarmed that no new people were coming. In our big church, we had visitors every week.

It was at this time that I heard a segment from one of my husband's tapes as we were traveling down the interstate. The speaker asked the question, "If God would send a visitor to your church this Sunday, are you ready for him?" The speaker went on to compare the visitor's coming to the birth of a child. When we know that a child is going to be born into our home, we prepare. We buy clothes, we prepare a room, we prepare a bed, and we prepare our life-style to adjust to the birth of that child.

The speaker really caught my attention when he said that if we failed to make all the preparations, the baby would still be born; but if we failed to nurture that baby, feed it, and love it, after a few days it would die. He went on to say that the same is true in many of our churches. We may plan for the visitor's arrival and greet him royally when he attends; but unless we commit ourselves to his nurture until he is a mature Christian and integrated into the life of the church, we have let a newborn die of neglect. The tape ended, "If I were God, how many newborns do you think I'd send to your church if you consistently had a high mortality rate?" I was numb.

In the large church I could assume that the people who had the "gift of greeting" were taking care of the area of inviting and nurturing the newcomers, while I was busy with my gifts. In this church, it was as though God said, "If I am to send

71

newcomers to your church, you are going to have to stop assuming that someone else has the gift of greeting. I want you to do it." I agreed to expand my realm of gifts and allow God to help me invite the newcomer, prepare for his coming, and nurture him when he arrived. I wanted our little church to grow.

I'm sure that you want your church to grow too. Whether your church is small, large, or in between, your congregation needs a greeting ministry to care for the newcomers: the seedlings, the newborns. And your greeting ministry needs your involvement.

Don't stand idly by while newborns die at your church doors. Aggressively do your best to prepare for those newcomers' visits. Give them a royal welcome that will cause them to want to return. Then go one step further—plan for the nurture of the newcomers. Devise ways to keep in contact with the newcomers until they are fully integrated into the life of your church.

Your newcomers are tender shoots, newborn babies that are depending on the loving care of your greeting ministry. Surround them with that tender loving care until at last they are feeling at home in your church.

A GREETER'S PRAYER

May those who come inside our church,
Whom I will greet
See Christ in all I do and say.
And remind me, Lord, that
Newcomers are not just
People who chose to worship here today,
But they are souls
Whom You have sent by me
In hopes that they might be saved.

"Let them know, Let them know . . ."
How often I've sung those words
And thought of Africa
Or downtown Detroit.
But Lord, let me see my neighborhood,
My town and its suburbs
As the mission field
Where millions are dying without knowing
That You care.

I'll not be just a greeter or an usher
For my church,
But Your greeter, Your usher,
At Your house.
May I greet every person with
Prayer and sincerity,
Seeing this greeting ministry
As an opportunity
To introduce newcomers to You.

Group Interaction

1. Discuss the four fellowship ideas: Visitation, Fellowship Dinners, Fellowship Nights, and the Open Home Committee. Which would be effective in your local situation? Do you have some other ideas for a fellowship ministry? If possible set a date for your fellowship ministry and appoint someone to organize that fellowship idea.

2. How well is your church equipped to care for your "newborns"? What is your mortality rate? What can you do to help lower that rate?

3. What is God saying to you about your present "realm of gifts"? Is He wanting to expand your area of ministry?

4. Review the Time Line Checklist. (See Appendix A.) Make greeter position assignments and delegate all other areas that still need attention.

5. Ask your pastor to come for at least the last few minutes of your session to pray a special prayer for each of the greeters, their ministry, and the ministry of your church to your community.

Appendixes

TIME LINE CHECKLIST

PRIOR TO SESSION 1

1. Choose or invite all who are interested in the ministry of greeting and ushering to gather for the purpose of instruction and encouragement.

2. Order a copy of *The Winning Welcome* for each person attending the class.

3. Determine how this material will be presented: 5 one-hour sessions, 3 half-hour sessions, 2 Saturday mornings, or other times, and reserve these dates on your church calendar.

4. Begin enthusiastic advertising of the class.

WEEK 1

1. Candidly evaluate your present organization, or lack of such.

WEEK 2

1. Decide where you will need greeters and ushers and determine some of your unique needs of greeting and ushering.

2. Design a greeter assignment sheet that covers your greeting and ushering needs, using the sample in Appendix D.

WEEK 3

1. Evaluate the decor of your sanctuary and entryway. Does your building and do your greeters say, "Welcome"? Is there any clutter that can easily be eliminated or minor redecorating that could provide a more pleasant atmosphere?

2. Make tentative assignments for each greeter and usher position.

3. Order name tags for the greeters and ushers.

4. Order visitor I.D. (See Appendix C for suggestions.)

5. Decide on the type of visitor's cards and/or register that you will use. Order what is needed.

WEEK 4

1. Evaluate your brochure collection and need for a map of your facilities.

WEEK 5

1. Choose one fellowship idea to initiate your new or renewed vision for greeting. Set a date. Appoint someone to organize and advertise it.

2. Review your strategy and confirm the assigned greeter and usher positions. Evaluate your greeting crew to determine whether or not child care is needed for the early arrival time of greeters and ushers. If so, make the necessary arrangements.

3. Schedule a devotional and prayer time for the greeters prior to your target beginning date.

WEEK 10 (Sooner if Necessary)

1. Meet again to evaluate your organization.

2. Make revisions wherever necessary.

Thereafter, meet at least once every three months, preferably in a potluck or at least a fellowship setting, to share the joys and frustrations of this ministry. Regroup, reorganize, but never retreat.

DESIGNING A WELCOME CENTER

This 6' x 3' Welcome Center is adequate for two greeters to use simultaneously. The ledge is 10" wide and allows sufficient writing space. The height of 3'6" is a comfortable writing level. This ledge is also large enough to hold the register, the bro-

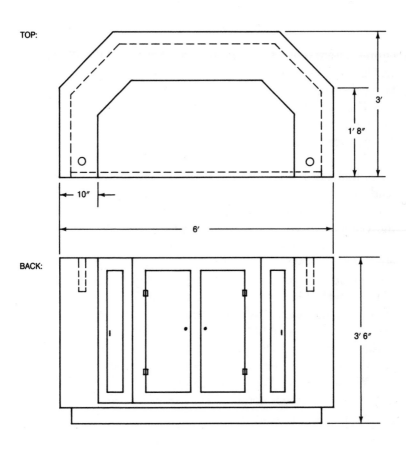

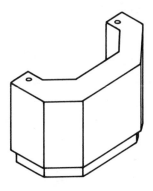

chures, and the maps. The ridge at the bottom of the Welcome Center hides the casters that were installed to make the center portable.

The storage space on the back side of the Welcome Center can be locked, giving a secure place for all supplies, the greeters' handbags, and so on.

The holes constructed on each side of the ledge are for poles that can hold a sign the width of the center, which can read either "Welcome" or "Welcome Center." This sign is especially helpful if you have an excessively crowded foyer or if the visibility of your Welcome Center is poor.

I have seen Welcome Centers constructed in many different shapes and sizes. I saw one that was constructed in a complete circle with part of the ledge lifting to permit the entrance of the greeter. I have also seen centers that looked like a counter, a table, or a desk. I've seen them made of plywood covered with carpet and a table covered with a lace cloth. My church chose to have a church furniture company design one to match our sanctuary furniture. It is less costly than you would expect.

Whatever your Welcome Center is like, make it a visibly attractive, functional center that is comfortable for both the greeter and the newcomer.

Appendix C

The heart on the sample Welcome Card is an embroidered appliqué with an adhesive backing so that visitors can place it

WELCOME *TO A CHURCH*
WITH A HEART

Church Name

OUR CHURCH CAN BE YOUR HOME

(reverse of welcome card)

This heart is yours to welcome you;
We pray that in some way
The love of God will warm your heart
As you worship here today.

REV. RICHARD A. BUSHEY
Pastor
546-1611

REV. GEORGE COOK   KENNETH RANKIN
Minister of Visitation   *Minister of Youth*
1-313-498-3291   548-3173

GARY GRIFFIN   MRS. CAROL AHNERT
Minister of Music   *Office Secretary*
546-1539   546-5500

Our staff is here to serve you.

on their clothes without the use of pins. (See NPH Master Buying Guide for appliqués available.) Or there is a way to give this a personal touch. A lady in one of our churches crocheted hearts for our newcomers and used two-sided tape in place of the adhesive.

Appendix D

GREETER AND USHER
POSITION PREFERENCE FORM

Although the final decision for placement will be left to the Greeter/Usher Committee chairperson and the pastor, please complete the following form. To aid in the placement, please list three positions where you would be willing to serve. Please mark them in the order of your preference.

1 = 1st choice   2 = 2nd choice   3 = 3rd choice

_____ Parking Lot Greeter

_____ Portico Center Greeter

_____ Door Greeter

_____ Welcome Center Host/Hostess

_____ Welcome Center Greeter/Secretary

_____ Escort Greeter

_____ Sunday School Class Greeter

_____ Usher

_____ Doorkeeper

INTEREST QUESTIONNAIRE

Name:_____ Phone:_____

Address:_____

Please check the interest groups about which you would like more information.

_____ Women's Share Group

_____ Women's Bible Study

_____ Women's Fellowship Nights

_____ Women's Craft Classes

_____ Men's Prayer Fellowship

_____ Men's Monthly Fellowship

_____ Softball League (check preference)

    _____ Men's Tournament Team

    _____ Men's Fun Team

    _____ Father/Son Team

    _____ Mother/Daughter Team

_____ Golf League (check preference)

    _____ Men/Boys' League

    _____ Women's League

    _____ Couples' League

Please check the ministries in which you would consider participating as openings permit.

_____ Choir

_____ Orchestra

_____ Piano Accompanist

_____ Usher/Greeter

_____ Sunday School teacher (check age-group preference)

     _____ Nursery   _____ Middle School

     _____ Preschool   _____ Senior High

     _____ Elementary   _____ Adult

_____ Chaperon for teen outings

_____ Nursery duty

Please check the appropriate boxes:

☐ I would like more information about the church history class that is presented quarterly.

☐ I would like to schedule my portrait to be taken to appear on the Get-Acquainted Portrait Board in the foyer.

☐ I have questions about the church and would like a call from the pastor or an elder.

Appendix F

Our Get-Acquainted Portrait Board is constructed of colored poster board, 3'4" x 2'8". It is trimmed with a lace border. The words "Welcome New Church Families" is written in gold, outlined in black. The portraits are attached by balancing them between decorative pins.

A permanent bulletin board could also serve the same purpose.